ONE2ONE

ONE2ONE

Personal Discipleship Guide

EVERY NATION
R E S O U R C E S

ONE 2 ONE

© 1996–2019 by Steve Murrell
All rights reserved.
Published by Every Nation Churches & Ministries
P.O. Box 1787, Brentwood, TN 37024-1787, USA
Email: communications@everynation.org

First published with ten chapters in 1996.
Second edition published with twelve chapters in 2000.
Third edition published with six chapters in 2009.
Fourth edition published with seven chapters in 2013.
Fifth edition published in ESV in 2014.
Sixth edition published in 2015.

Scripture quotations are from The Holy Bible, English Standard Version® (ESV®), Copyright © 2001 by Crossway, a publishing ministry of Good News Publishers. Used by permission. All rights reserved.

Printed in the United States of America.

CONTENTS

THE RIGHT START

From 1974 to 1979, a young upstart Presbyterian youth pastor named Ron invaded local high schools in my hometown of Jackson, Mississippi, boldly sharing the gospel one-on-one with anyone who would listen, and with some who wouldn't. Over the years, countless teenagers heard and understood God's plan of salvation for the first time. Hundreds responded. Many went on to serve the Lord in full-time ministry as church planters, youth ministers, pastors, and missionaries.

I'm one of those who heard the gospel for the first time through Ron back in the mid-seventies. However, my first response to Ron and his gospel was not to repent, but to run. I ran from Ron, from his disciples, and from God. I ran for about six months, avoiding Ron the best I could. It was a difficult task as he seemed to show up everywhere. He was at every football and basketball game. He was in the school halls, in the cafeteria, in the parking lot. He and his band of disciples were always inviting me to another retreat, another Bible study, another prayer meeting, another youth night at the church. Finally, in November of 1975, I responded to the gospel. I repented and put my faith in Christ alone.

Fortunately, it didn't end there. Ron wasn't content just to carve a notch in his well-worn Bible to represent yet another soul saved. Since he was not out to save souls, but to make disciples, his work with me was just beginning. He added me to one of his famous "action groups" where about eight of us met together weekly and learned to walk with God.

I believe in one-to-one evangelism, one-to-one follow-up, and one-to-one discipleship. Here's why. Ron shared the gospel with me. I didn't respond. I ran. Ron ran after me. For six months, he ran after me, preaching to me and praying for me. He just wouldn't go away. That's one-to-one follow-up.

After I responded to the gospel, Ron began to disciple me in a small group. He taught me how to study and live the Bible. He taught me how to pray. He taught me how to share my faith and how to make disciples. That's one-to-one discipleship.

Personal follow-up and discipleship. That's the Great Commission. That's what this little book is all about.

ONE 2 ONE was written as a simple tool to aid in personal follow-up and discipleship. It's a guide. It cannot make a disciple, but it can help you make one. Most importantly, it helps a new disciple get the right start.

Steve Murrell
President, Every Nation Churches & Ministries

GETTING STARTED

And Jesus said to them, "Follow me, and I will make you become fishers of men."

MARK 1:17

These five steps will get you off to the right START, as you follow Christ.

S top trusting in yourself and your own good works, and start trusting in Christ alone for salvation.

> *[8]For by grace you have been saved through faith. And this is not your own doing; it is the gift of God, [9]not a result of works, so that no one may boast.*
>
> EPHESIANS 2:8, 9

T urn away from everything the Bible calls sin.

> *But God's firm foundation stands, bearing this seal: "The Lord knows those who are his," and, "Let everyone who names the name of the Lord depart from iniquity."*
>
> 2 TIMOTHY 2:19

Attend a small group for personal discipleship and weekly worship services.

> *²⁴And let us consider how to stir up one another to love and good works, ²⁵not neglecting to meet together, as is the habit of some, but encouraging one another, and all the more as you see the Day drawing near.*
>
> HEBREWS 10:24, 25

Read and obey your Bible every day.

> *"This Book of the Law shall not depart from your mouth, but you shall meditate on it day and night, so that you may be careful to do according to all that is written in it. For then you will make your way prosperous, and then you will have good success."*
>
> JOSHUA 1:8

Tell others about your new relationship with Christ.

> *¹⁹And he did not permit him but said to him, "Go home to your friends and tell them how much the Lord has done for you, and how he has had mercy on you." ²⁰And he went away and began to proclaim in the Decapolis how much Jesus had done for him, and everyone marveled.*
>
> MARK 5:19, 20

1 SALVATION

A New Start

> Therefore, if anyone is in Christ, he is a new creation. The old has passed away; behold, the new has come.
>
> 2 CORINTHIANS 5:17

A new creation. A fresh start. For all of us who have ever wished we could start over, this is good news. However, before we can really appreciate this good news, we need to understand exactly why we need to start over. Why do we need to become *a new creation*? Why do we need salvation?

THE PROBLEM:
Separation Because of Our Sin

There is an immeasurable gap separating God and man. The cause of this eternal separation between God and man is sin.

Have you ever felt distant from God? We all have. Feeling far from God is very common. Many who sense this vast separation suppose that if they meditate harder, learn more about their religion, or just step into a religious sanctuary, they would be closer to God. But since our separation from God is not physical or intellectual, neither meditation nor knowledge can bring us any closer to God. What causes the separation between God and man?

> ¹*Behold, the Lord's hand is not shortened, that it cannot save, or his ear dull, that it cannot hear;* ²*but your iniquities have made a separation between you and your God, and your sins have hidden his face from you so that he does not hear.*
>
> ISAIAH 59:1, 2

The separation between God and man is a moral separation. God is holy; man is not. God is good; man is not. God is just; man is not. All men have sinned; therefore, all are eternally separated from God. All will suffer the consequences of sin, which is eternal death.

> *. . . for all have sinned and fall short of the glory of God . . .*
>
> ROMANS 3:23

> *For the wages of sin is death, but the free gift of God is eternal life in Christ Jesus our Lord.*
>
> ROMANS 6:23

THE SOLUTION:
God's Sacrifice and Substitution

The justice of God demands a sacrifice for man's sin. Jesus Christ became that sacrifice and paid the penalty for our sin at the cross.

Since God is holy, righteous, and just, He could not allow sin to go unpunished. Since He is loving and compassionate, He did not want all of mankind to be eternally separated from Him. The divine solution to this problem was for Jesus, God's only Son, to become the sacrifice for sin.

> *[26]. . . for then he would have had to suffer repeatedly since the foundation of the world. But as it is, he has appeared once for all at the end of the ages to put away sin by the sacrifice of himself. [27]And just as it is appointed for man to die once, and after that comes judgment, [28]so Christ, having been offered once to bear the sins of many, will appear a second time, not to deal with sin but to save those who are eagerly waiting for him.*
>
> HEBREWS 9:26–28

What exactly happened on the cross? Through His death on the cross, Jesus took our place and our punishment. He exchanged His righteousness for our sin. He took our curse and gave us His blessings. Because of His sinless life, Jesus was the only one qualified to pay the penalty for man's sin and to bridge the gap between God and man.

> *For our sake he made him to be sin who knew no sin, so that in him we might become the righteousness of God.*
>
> 2 CORINTHIANS 5:21

> *Christ redeemed us from the curse of*
> *the law by becoming a curse for us—for it is*
> *written, "Cursed is everyone who is hanged on*
> *a tree" . . .*
>
> GALATIANS 3:13

THE RESULT:
Our Salvation and Reconciliation

Christ died on the cross so that we could receive forgiveness for our sins, be reconciled to God, and have eternal life.

We have all sinned against a holy and righteous God. The penalty for sin is eternal separation from God in hell. God is just and must punish sin. He is also loving and does not want us to go to hell forever. Therefore, He sent His Son, Jesus Christ, to pay the penalty for sin by dying on the cross. Because of His sinless life, death could not hold Jesus. He was raised from the dead on the third day. In Christ, we experience forgiveness for our sins and eternal life. In Him we are restored to right standing before God and given new life as His children.

> *"For God so loved the world, that he gave his*
> *only Son, that whoever believes in him should*
> *not perish but have eternal life."*
>
> JOHN 3:16

> *In him we have redemption through his blood,*
> *the forgiveness of our trespasses, according to*
> *the riches of his grace . . .*
>
> EPHESIANS 1:7

> *But now in Christ Jesus you who once were*
> *far off have been brought near by the blood*
> *of Christ.*
>
> EPHESIANS 2:13

THE RESPONSE:
Receive God's Gift by Faith

We receive salvation when we stop trusting in ourselves and put our trust in what Christ did for us.

Our salvation is a result of God's grace. It is based on what Jesus did for us on the cross. It has nothing to do with what we do for Him. We cannot save ourselves or earn God's approval through the good works we do. We are saved by God's grace when we realize our need for a Savior, turn from sin, and receive Jesus Christ as Lord and Savior, putting our trust in Him alone for salvation.

> *[9]. . . if you confess with your mouth that*
> *Jesus is Lord and believe in your heart that*
> *God raised him from the dead, you will be*
> *saved. [10]For with the heart one believes and*
> *is justified, and with the mouth one confesses*
> *and is saved.*
>
> ROMANS 10:9, 10

> *[8]For by grace you have been saved through*
> *faith. And this is not your own doing; it is the*
> *gift of God, [9]not a result of works, so that no*
> *one may boast.*
>
> EPHESIANS 2:8, 9

Personal Application

- Have you stopped trusting in yourself and started trusting in Christ alone for salvation?

  _____

  _____

- Have you turned away from all known sin?

  _____

  _____

- Have you confessed Jesus as the Lord and Master of your life?

  _____

  _____

- Are you willing to follow and obey Him for the rest of your life?

  _____

  _____

PRAYER FOR SALVATION

> *Heavenly Father . . . I acknowledge that the*
> *separation between us . . . is because of my sin . . .*
> *I confess that I have sinned . . . and have fallen far*
> *short of Your glory . . . I thank You that You sent Your*
> *Son, Jesus . . . to pay the penalty for my sin . . .*
> *I believe that He died on the cross for me . . .*
> *I believe that You raised Him from the dead . . .*
> *I am sorry for my sins . . . and I ask You to forgive*
> *and cleanse me . . . I want to turn away from*
> *everything the Bible calls sin . . . and receive Jesus*
> *as my Lord, Master, and Savior . . . help me to love,*
> *serve, and obey You . . . for the rest of my life . . .*
> *in Jesus' name . . . Amen!*

A NEW LIFE

If you have sincerely prayed that prayer, the Bible
promises that the old has passed away and the new has
come! The next six lessons will introduce you to some of
the new things that have come.

2 LORDSHIP

A New Master

> "Let all the house of Israel therefore know for certain that God has made him both Lord and Christ, this Jesus whom you crucified."
>
> ACTS 2:36

Lordship is one of the central messages of the Bible. Jesus is referred to as *Lord* 100 times in the book of Acts and 622 times in the whole New Testament, while being referred to as *Savior* only twice in Acts and twenty-four times in the New Testament. The biblical emphasis is overwhelmingly on the concept of Lordship. Lord means *master*, the one who calls the shots, the one who makes the decisions.

LORDSHIP AND SALVATION

The starting point of salvation is the acknowledgment of the Lordship of Christ. Confessing Jesus is Lord implies a submission to His Lordship in every area of life. If Jesus is not Lord of all, He is not Lord at all. We do not have the option of receiving Him as Savior and not as Lord. Salvation is an all-or-nothing proposal.

> *. . . if you confess with your mouth that Jesus is Lord and believe in your heart that God raised him from the dead, you will be saved.*
>
> ROMANS 10:9

LORDSHIP DEMANDS OBEDIENCE

Anyone who claims Christ as their Lord is expected to do what He says. Intellectual faith and empty confession is not enough. If we say Christ is our Lord, our lifestyle should back up our claim.

> *"Why do you call me 'Lord, Lord,' and not do what I tell you?"*
>
> LUKE 6:46
>
> *"Not everyone who says to me, 'Lord, Lord,' will enter the kingdom of heaven, but the one who does the will of my Father who is in heaven."*
>
> MATTHEW 7:21

LORDSHIP BEGINS IN THE HEART

Submitting to Christ as Lord is not about following a set of religious rules and traditions. Rather, Lordship is a matter of the heart. Lordship begins as an internal submission of the heart. If it is genuine, it will eventually manifest itself in outward obedience.

> *. . . but in your hearts honor Christ the Lord as holy . . .*
>
> 1 PETER 3:15

LORDSHIP IS A CONTINUOUS WALK

We begin our Christian life by acknowledging that Jesus is Lord. We must continue to walk under His Lordship for the rest of our lives. Lordship is not having a one-time experience with God, but developing a lifetime walk with God. The more we know Him, the more we submit to Him.

> *Therefore, as you received Christ Jesus the Lord, so walk in him . . .*
>
> COLOSSIANS 2:6

Personal Application

- Are there areas in your life that you have not yet submitted to the Lordship of Jesus Christ?

  _____

  _____

- Are your relationships under His Lordship?

  _____

  _____

- Are your finances under His Lordship?

  _____

  _____

- Is your time submitted to His Lordship?

  _____

  _____

3 REPENTANCE

A New Direction

> And Peter said to them, "Repent and be baptized every one of you in the name of Jesus Christ for the forgiveness of your sins, and you will receive the gift of the Holy Spirit."
>
> ACTS 2:38

Driving a car in the wrong direction on a one-way street is foolish and dangerous. Some drive the wrong way out of ignorance; others out of rebellion. There is a spiritual parallel. Whether out of ignorance or rebellion, we are all on a dangerous one-way street that will ultimately lead to eternal separation from God. Until we turn around (repent) and begin following Christ, every step we take is a step in the wrong direction—a step away from God.

REPENTANCE, GRIEF, AND FRUIT

Real repentance begins when we are truly sorry for our sins. This *godly grief* makes no excuses, takes full responsibility, and never places blame on people, society, or circumstances. It acknowledges that our sin is primarily against God. Godly grief produces true repentance and a changed life.

*For godly grief produces a repentance that
leads to salvation without regret, whereas
worldly grief produces death.*

2 CORINTHIANS 7:10

*I acknowledged my sin to you, and I did not
cover my iniquity; I said, "I will confess my
transgressions to the Lord," and you forgave
the iniquity of my sin.*

PSALM 32:5

On the other hand, *worldly grief* only produces excuses.
While godly grief is having a broken heart when we
realize we have offended a holy God, worldly grief is
being sorry we got caught, or being sorry we have to
suffer the consequences of sin. The ultimate difference
between godly grief and worldly grief is the fruit. Worldly
grief never produces the fruit of a changed life; it only
produces spiritual death.

*". . . they should repent and turn to God,
performing deeds in keeping with
their repentance."*

ACTS 26:20

"Bear fruit in keeping with repentance."

MATTHEW 3:8

REPENTANCE AND FORGIVENESS

The parable of the prodigal son in Luke 15:11–24 is a
beautiful picture of true repentance. The wayward son
came to his senses, turned his back on his folly, and

returned to his father. He made a 180-degree turn, walking away from his former life of sin and rebellion. His father forgave him for his offenses and received him back. In the same way, our heavenly Father is faithful to forgive us when we turn to Him and repent of our sins.

> [19]*"Repent therefore, and turn back, that your sins may be blotted out* [20]*that times of refreshing may come from the presence of the Lord . . ."*
>
> ACTS 3:19, 20

Ever had a stain on your shirt that you couldn't wash out? Imagine a stain remover that would not only remove the stain, but would make the shirt just like new again. That's what happens when we repent and receive Jesus as our Lord and Savior. He not only cleans sin's stain of guilt and shame from our hearts, He gives us a new heart.

> *If we confess our sins, he is faithful and just to forgive us our sins and to cleanse us from all unrighteousness.*
>
> 1 JOHN 1:9

THE IMPORTANCE OF FORGIVING OTHERS

Just as we received forgiveness from God, we are now commanded by God to forgive those who have sinned against us.

> *21 Then Peter came up and said to him, "Lord, how often will my brother sin against me, and I forgive him? As many as seven times?" 22 Jesus said to him, "I do not say to you seven times, but seventy-seven times."*
>
> MATTHEW 18:21, 22

But if we refuse to forgive, the Bible says that we will be defiled by a *root of bitterness*, which causes trouble.

> *See to it that no one fails to obtain the grace of God; that no "root of bitterness" springs up and causes trouble, and by it many become defiled . . .*
>
> HEBREWS 12:15

NO REGRET

Repentance is turning away from sin and turning to God. It means we stop trusting in our own good deeds and religious activity and start trusting in Christ alone. We were going in the wrong direction; now we are going in the right direction. We were running from God; now we are walking with Him. Repentance is the starting point of a new life. Repentance takes us off the treadmill of a self-centered life and puts us on the fast track of God's glorious purpose for our lives. Turning to God means no looking back and no regrets.

> *For godly grief produces a repentance that leads to salvation without regret . . .*
>
> 2 CORINTHIANS 7:10

Personal Application

- Is your life going in a new direction?

  _____

  _____

- Are there sinful areas in your life that are still
  a struggle?

  _____

  _____

- Are there areas of intense temptation or consistent
  weakness that you need prayer for?

  _____

  _____

- Are there sins that you have turned away from, yet
  you still feel condemned about?

  _____

  _____

4 BAPTISM

A New Life

> [38]And Peter said to them, "Repent and be baptized every one of you in the name of Jesus Christ for the forgiveness of your sins, and you will receive the gift of the Holy Spirit. . . ." [41]So those who received his word were baptized, and there were added that day about three thousand souls.
>
> ACTS 2:38, 41

When the crowd asked Peter what they should do in response to his sermon, he gave them a threefold answer: repent, be baptized, and receive the gift of the Holy Spirit. Thousands responded and were added to the fellowship of believers. The biblical pattern is that everyone who is baptized is also added. Every baptized disciple is expected to become an active member of a local fellowship.

WATER BAPTISM

In water baptism, we publicly identify with what Christ did for us on the cross. It is not a means for salvation, but an act of faith and obedience after believing the gospel and turning to God.

The Bible presents several illustrations to help us understand water baptism. One of these is a burial and resurrection. Paul compares a Christian baptism to a burial. In order to be buried, a person must first die. In the same way, the prerequisite for baptism is death to sin. After we are buried in baptism, then we are raised to live a new life.

> ¹What shall we say then? Are we to continue in sin that grace may abound? ²By no means! How can we who died to sin still live in it? ³Do you not know that all of us who have been baptized into Christ Jesus were baptized into his death? ⁴We were buried therefore with him by baptism into death, in order that, just as Christ was raised from the dead by the glory of the Father, we too might walk in newness of life.
>
> ROMANS 6:1–4

We see, then, that water baptism shows the old life being put away, and a new life emerging in obedience to Christ.

THE BAPTISM OF THE HOLY SPIRIT

It is impossible to live the Christian life apart from the power and presence of the Holy Spirit. Jesus promised that the Holy Spirit would come to lead us into all truth.

> [7]*"Nevertheless, I tell you the truth: it is to your advantage that I go away, for if I do not go away, the Helper will not come to you. But if I go, I will send him to you. . . . [13]When the Spirit of truth comes, he will guide you into all the truth, for he will not speak on his own authority, but whatever he hears he will speak, and he will declare to you the things that are to come."*

JOHN 16:7, 13

The Holy Spirit empowers us to be effective witnesses. A witness is one who not only tells the truth, but also lives the truth. As His witnesses, the Holy Spirit helps us to do what we cannot do on our own—to boldly proclaim and live out the truth about God.

> *"But you will receive power when the Holy Spirit has come upon you, and you will be my witnesses in Jerusalem and in all Judea and Samaria, and to the end of the earth."*

ACTS 1:8

HOW TO RECEIVE THE BAPTISM OF THE HOLY SPIRIT

The baptism of the Holy Spirit is a gift promised for every believer, not just for those present during Pentecost. In Peter's sermon, he told us how we can receive the gift of the Holy Spirit.

> [38]And Peter said to them, "Repent and be baptized every one of you in the name of Jesus Christ for the forgiveness of your sins, and you will receive the gift of the Holy Spirit. [39]For the promise is for you and for your children and for all who are far off, everyone whom the Lord our God calls to himself."
>
> ACTS 2:38, 39

In order to receive the baptism of the Holy Spirit, we must ask—and we must ask in faith.

> "If you then, who are evil, know how to give good gifts to your children, how much more will the heavenly Father give the Holy Spirit to those who ask him!"
>
> LUKE 11:13

Many disciples in the New Testament received the baptism of the Holy Spirit through the laying on of hands.

> Then they laid their hands on them and they received the Holy Spirit.
>
> ACTS 8:17

SPIRITUAL GIFTS

The baptism of the Holy Spirit is accompanied by the manifestation of spiritual gifts. In the biblical accounts of the baptism in the Holy Spirit, the most common spiritual gift manifested is the gift of tongues.

And they were all filled with the Holy Spirit and began to speak in other tongues as the Spirit gave them utterance.

ACTS 2:4

And when Paul had laid his hands on them, the Holy Spirit came on them, and they began speaking in tongues and prophesying.

ACTS 19:6

EMPOWERED TO BE A WITNESS

Jesus promised to fill us with the Holy Spirit so we can be effective witnesses. The Holy Spirit empowers us to proclaim the gospel wherever we go.

"But you will receive power when the Holy Spirit has come upon you, and you will be my witnesses in Jerusalem and in all Judea and Samaria, and to the end of the earth."

ACTS 1:8

Personal Application

- Have you repented of your sins?

  _____

  _____

- Have you put your trust in Christ alone for salvation?

  _____

  _____

- Have you been baptized in water since you repented? Would you like to get water baptized?

  _____

  _____

- Have you received the baptism of the Holy Spirit? Would you like to have someone pray with you to receive the baptism of the Holy Spirit?

  _____

  _____

5 DEVOTION

New Disciplines

> And they devoted themselves to the apostles' teaching and the fellowship, to the breaking of bread and the prayers.

ACTS 2:42

What made the early church vibrant and healthy was their devotion to God. Because they were devoted to grow in their relationship with Him, they developed disciplines that expressed this devotion. Two of these vital disciplines are reading the Bible and praying.

WORD

More than just a random collection of stories, poems, and letters, the Bible is the inspired written Word of God. We must follow the example of Job who valued God's Word more than food.

> *"I have not departed from the commandment of his lips; I have treasured the words of his mouth more than my portion of food."*

JOB 23:12

Before turning to Christ, we lived by the world's standards. Now we accept the Bible as the final authority for what we believe and how we live.

God's Word is the ultimate and absolute standard for every area of life.

The measure of our spiritual progress is not how much of the Bible we know, but how much we obey. Those who constantly learn but fail to obey end up deceiving themselves.

> *But be doers of the word, and not hearers only, deceiving yourselves.*
>
> JAMES 1:22

The Bible is our key to spiritual growth. It is also how we resist temptation, how we become successful, and how we can know God's will for our lives.

> *²Like newborn infants, long for the pure spiritual milk, that by it you may grow up into salvation—³if indeed you have tasted that the Lord is good.*
>
> 1 PETER 2:2, 3

> *⁹How can a young man keep his way pure? By guarding it according to your word. . . . ¹¹I have stored up your word in my heart, that I might not sin against you.*
>
> PSALM 119:9, 11

> *"This Book of the Law shall not depart from your mouth, but you shall meditate on it day and night, so that you may be careful to do according to all that is written in it. For then you will make your way prosperous, and then you will have good success."*
>
> JOSHUA 1:8

Do not be conformed to this world, but be transformed by the renewal of your mind, that by testing you may discern what is the will of God, what is good and acceptable and perfect.

ROMANS 12:2

PRAYER

Christianity is more than just a religion. It is first and foremost a relationship with God. The foundation of any healthy relationship is communication. The better the communication, the better the relationship will be. God talks to us in many ways but primarily through His Word, the Bible. We talk to Him through prayer. We learn to listen to the sound of God's voice in our lives when we read His Word. He listens to us when we pray. We respond to His Word with action. He responds to our prayers with action.

Jesus is our best example for prayer. By observing His personal prayer life, we can learn how to have an intimate time of connection with the Father.

Now Jesus was praying in a certain place, and when he finished, one of his disciples said to him, "Lord, teach us to pray, as John taught his disciples."

LUKE 11:1

Jesus told us not to pray like the hypocrites and those who don't know God.

> [5]*"And when you pray, you must not be like the hypocrites. For they love to stand and pray in the synagogues and at the street corners, that they may be seen by others. Truly, I say to you, they have received their reward. . . . [7]And when you pray, do not heap up empty phrases as the Gentiles do, for they think that they will be heard for their many words. [8]Do not be like them, for your Father knows what you need before you ask him."*

MATTHEW 6:5, 7, 8

Jesus told us to pray to the Father, not to the mother, saints, or angels. We are to pray through Jesus, because He is the only way to the Father.

> *"But when you pray, go into your room and shut the door and pray to your Father who is in secret. And your Father who sees in secret will reward you."*

MATTHEW 6:6

> *For there is one God, and there is one mediator between God and men, the man Christ Jesus . . .*

1 TIMOTHY 2:5

> *Jesus said to him, "I am the way, and the truth, and the life. No one comes to the Father except through me."*

JOHN 14:6

Jesus taught His disciples to pray for God's will to be done, provision, forgiveness, victory over temptation, and protection from the devil's schemes.

> *9Pray then like this: "Our Father in heaven, hallowed be your name. 10Your kingdom come, your will be done, on earth as it is in heaven. 11Give us this day our daily bread, 12and forgive us our debts, as we also have forgiven our debtors. 13And lead us not into temptation, but deliver us from evil."*
>
> MATTHEW 6:9–13

As we read and obey the Word, and as we pray and trust God with our lives, let us not forget that God really answers prayer. The more specific the prayers, the more specific the answers will be. The secret is to pray according to His will. We know His will by knowing His Word. Therefore, as we pray according to His Word, we know He will answer.

> *14And this is the confidence that we have toward him, that if we ask anything according to his will he hears us. 15And if we know that he hears us in whatever we ask, we know that we have the requests that we have asked of him.*
>
> 1 JOHN 5:14, 15

Personal Application

- Do you have a set time and place for daily Bible reading and prayer?

  _____

  _____

- Are you involved in a discipleship group?

  _____

  _____

- Have you forgiven all who have sinned against you?

  _____

  _____

- Begin praying for your _daily bread_.

  _____

  _____

6 CHURCH

New Relationships

> [16]Simon Peter replied, "You are the Christ, the Son of the living God." [17]And Jesus answered him, "Blessed are you, Simon Bar-Jonah! For flesh and blood has not revealed this to you, but my Father who is in heaven. [18]And I tell you, you are Peter, and on this rock I will build my church, and the gates of hell shall not prevail against it."
>
> MATTHEW 16:16–18

Through a revelation of the Holy Spirit, Peter confessed the true identity of Jesus, the Son of the living God. Jesus said this truth would be the foundation stone that His church would be built on. He also described the type of church He would build, a victorious church that would overcome the kingdom of darkness. Jesus and Paul used the word *church* in reference to the people of God. Church never referred to a religious building. Following are four benefits of being part of a local church.

FRIENDSHIP

Real friends. Everyone needs them. Few find them.
The best place to look for a real friend is in the church, the people of God. True friends are those who have our

best interest in mind. They stick with us through thick and thin. Real friends never lead us away from God. Instead, they provoke us to godliness.

> *A friend loves at all times, and a brother is born for adversity.*
>
> PROVERBS 17:17

> *A man of many companions may come to ruin, but there is a friend who sticks closer than a brother.*
>
> PROVERBS 18:24

FELLOWSHIP

If a piece of burning coal is removed from the fire, it will cool off. If it is put back in the middle of a pile of red-hot coals, it will burn again. The same is true of Christians. If a Christian is removed from fellowship with other red-hot Christians, he will cool off spiritually. If a Christian stays in fellowship, he will stay on fire for God.

> *[42]And they devoted themselves to the apostles' teaching and the fellowship, to the breaking of bread and the prayers. . . . [44]And all who believed were together and had all things in common. [45]And they were selling their possessions and belongings and distributing the proceeds to all, as any had need. [46]And day by day, attending the temple together and breaking bread in their homes, they received their food with glad and generous hearts . . .*
>
> ACTS 2:42, 44–46

> *Do not be unequally yoked with unbelievers.*
> *For what partnership has righteousness with*
> *lawlessness? Or what fellowship has light*
> *with darkness?*
>
> 2 CORINTHIANS 6:14

WORSHIP

God is looking for sincere worshipers. Worship is simply the expression of our love, devotion, and commitment to God.

> [23]*"But the hour is coming, and is now here,*
> *when the true worshipers will worship the*
> *Father in spirit and truth, for the Father is*
> *seeking such people to worship him.* [24]*God*
> *is spirit, and those who worship him must*
> *worship in spirit and truth."*
>
> JOHN 4:23, 24

DISCIPLESHIP

The last command Jesus gave His followers before He ascended to heaven was to go and make disciples, to baptize these disciples, and to teach them how to obey God's Word. Therefore, we should first be disciples or followers of Jesus, then we should teach others to follow Him.

19"Go therefore and make disciples of all nations, baptizing them in the name of the Father and of the Son and of the Holy Spirit, 20teaching them to observe all that I have commanded you. And behold, I am with you always, to the end of the age."

MATTHEW 28:19, 20

. . . and what you have heard from me in the presence of many witnesses entrust to faithful men who will be able to teach others also.

2 TIMOTHY 2:2

Personal Application

- Are you being discipled, either one-to-one or in a small group setting?

  _____

  _____

- Are you making disciples? Who are you teaching to obey God's Word?

  _____

  _____

- Are you an active member of a local church?

  _____

  _____

- Name three Christians you can call for help in case of a spiritual emergency.

  _____

  _____

7 DISCIPLESHIP

A New Mission

. . . but in your hearts honor Christ the Lord as holy, always being prepared to make a defense to anyone who asks you for a reason for the hope that is in you . . .

1 PETER 3:15

[18]As he was getting into the boat, the man who had been possessed with demons begged him that he might be with him. [19]And he did not permit him but said to him, "Go home to your friends and tell them how much the Lord has done for you, and how he has had mercy on you."

MARK 5:18, 19

If you were the doctor who discovered the miracle cure for cancer, wouldn't you want everyone to know about your discovery? You now have a miracle cure for something more deadly than cancer. You have the solution for sin. Making disciples starts with sharing the good news of God's solution for sin to your family and friends. In order to be prepared to tell others about the hope of salvation, we must learn how to give our testimony and preach the gospel. As we do this, we are starting to make disciples.

HOW TO GIVE YOUR TESTIMONY

In a court of law, a witness tells "the truth and nothing but the truth" about what he has seen, heard, and experienced. We are called to be God's witnesses. We are to tell the truth about what He has done for, in, and through us as we share our testimony.

Being a witness also demands that we live a life that testifies to the grace of our Lord Jesus. A witness is something we are, not something we do. We are to "be" witnesses. The only way we can be a witness is through the power of the Holy Spirit, who empowers us to boldly proclaim our testimony and the gospel.

The word of your testimony is powerful. It is a personal, irrefutable account of what Jesus has done for you and how He has changed your life. There are three parts to sharing your testimony, which is your two-minute miracle:

1. Briefly describe your life before Christ.

2. Carefully explain how you came to the point of submitting your life to Christ.

3. Joyfully describe your life since Jesus became Lord. Take more time to explain how your life has changed since you surrendered to Christ.

> *And they have conquered him by the blood of*
> *the Lamb and by the word of their testimony,*
> *for they loved not their lives even unto death.*
>
> REVELATION 12:11

HOW TO PREACH THE GOSPEL

The gospel is the power of God for the salvation of all who believe. It is the reason we engage culture and community, be a witness, and share our testimony.

> *For I am not ashamed of the gospel, for it is*
> *the power of God for salvation to everyone*
> *who believes, to the Jew first and also to*
> *the Greek.*
>
> ROMANS 1:16

Preach the gospel using two simple verses to your family and friends.

> *. . . for all have sinned and fall short of the*
> *glory of God . . .*
>
> ROMANS 3:23

Everyone has sinned. Sin is any act of disobedience or rebellion against God and, the truth is, not a single person on earth has perfectly obeyed God's commandments.

> *For the wages of sin is death, but the free gift*
> *of God is eternal life in Christ Jesus our Lord.*
>
> ROMANS 6:23

Since we have all sinned, we deserve death and are disqualified from even being in God's presence. The good news is salvation is that a free gift from God! Salvation is found in Christ alone because He died on the cross for us, in our place. We receive this free gift by faith as we trust in His finished work on the cross.

After you have presented the gospel to your family and friends, feel free to lead them in prayer.

HOW TO MAKE DISCIPLES

We make disciples as we introduce people to Jesus and teach them how to obey God's commands. Paul told Timothy to transfer everything he had learned to others who would be able to teach it to others. This is discipleship.

> [19]"Go therefore and make disciples of all nations, baptizing them in the name of the Father and of the Son and of the Holy Spirit, [20]teaching them to observe all that I have commanded you. And behold, I am with you always, to the end of the age."
>
> MATTHEW 28:19, 20
>
> . . . and what you have heard from me in the presence of many witnesses entrust to faithful men who will be able to teach others also.
>
> 2 TIMOTHY 2:2

Personal Application

- Is your life a witness for God?

  _____

  _____

- Share your two-minute miracle to whoever is going through this booklet with you.

  _____

  _____

- Pray for your family and friends who haven't heard the gospel yet. Believe God for opportunities to share the gospel with them.

  _____

  _____

- Go and make disciples!